# Trailblazers on LAND

by Charis Mather

Minneapolis, Minnesota

**Credits**
Images are courtesy of Shutterstock.com. With thanks to GettyImages, ThinkstockPhoto, and iStockphoto. Throughout – GoodStudio, mhatzapa. Cover – grynold, Hennadii H. 6–7, ClassicVector, Leonid studio, Macrovector; 8–9, osk1553, VectorShow, neftali; 10–11, Everett Collection; 12–13, Looper, MacroVector; 14–15, unknown (wiki commons); 16–17, KittyVector, Studio Tourne (WikiCommons), HappyPictures; 18–19, Anonymous (WikiCommons), Vika Kravchuk; 20–21, Jamling Tenzing Norgay (WikiCommons).

**Bearport Publishing Company Product Development Team**
President: Jen Jenson; Director of Product Development: Spencer Brinker; Managing Editor: Allison Juda; Associate Editor: Naomi Reich; Senior Designer: Colin O'Dea; Associate Designer: Elena Klinkner; Associate Designer: Kayla Eggert; Product Development Specialist: Anita Stasson

Library of Congress Cataloging-in-Publication Data is available at www.loc.gov or upon request from the publisher.

ISBN: 979-8-88509-956-1 (hardcover)
ISBN: 979-8-88822-131-0 (paperback)
ISBN: 979-8-88822-276-8 (ebook)

© 2024 BookLife Publishing
This edition is published by arrangement with BookLife Publishing.

North American adaptations © 2024 Bearport Publishing Company. All rights reserved. No part of this publication may be reproduced in whole or in part, stored in any retrieval system, or transmitted in any form or by any means, electronic, mechanical, photocopying, recording, or otherwise, without written permission from the publisher.

For more information, write to Bearport Publishing, 5357 Penn Avenue South, Minneapolis, MN 55419.

# CONTENTS

Our Greatest Adventures on Land . . . . . 4

Marco Polo . . . . . . . . . . . . . . . . . . . . . 6

Sacagawea . . . . . . . . . . . . . . . . . . . . 8

David Livingstone . . . . . . . . . . . . . . 10

Nellie Bly . . . . . . . . . . . . . . . . . . . 12

Gertrude Bell . . . . . . . . . . . . . . . . 14

Annie Londonderry . . . . . . . . . . . . . . 16

Roald Amundsen . . . . . . . . . . . . . . . 18

Edmund Hillary and Tenzing Norgay . . 20

Your Land Adventure . . . . . . . . . . . . 22

Glossary . . . . . . . . . . . . . . . . . . . . 24

Index . . . . . . . . . . . . . . . . . . . . . 24

# OUR GREATEST ADVENTURES ON LAND

What is the longest journey you have ever been on? In the past, traveling was difficult. Some places were not even on maps yet.

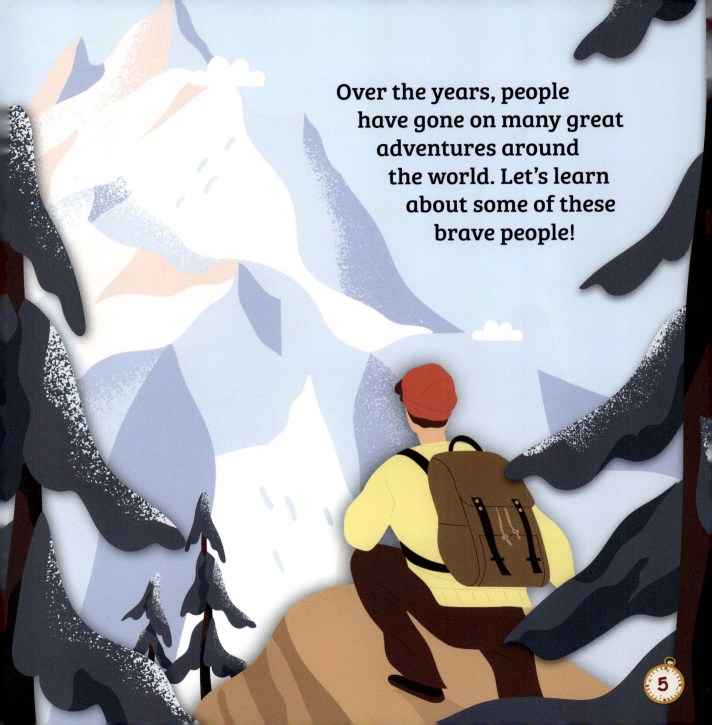

Over the years, people have gone on many great adventures around the world. Let's learn about some of these brave people!

# MARCO POLO

**Born: 1254**
**Died: 1324**

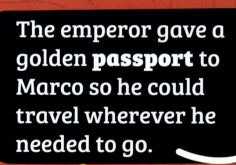

Marco Polo was an Italian explorer who traveled to learn about China. The **emperor** of China also wanted to learn more about Europe.

The emperor gave a golden **passport** to Marco so he could travel wherever he needed to go.

Marco traveled by camel. He was the first **European** to see some parts of China. Many people in Europe were amazed by the stories he brought back.

**Be Inspired!**
Try to learn something new wherever you go.

# SACAGAWEA

### Born: Around 1788   Died: Around 1812

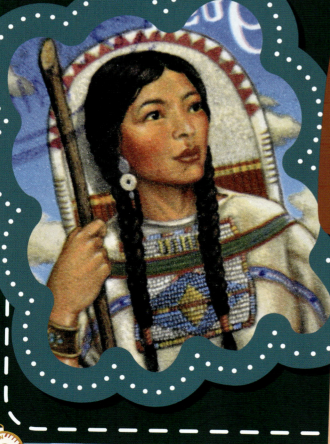

Sacagawea was a Native American woman who helped **explorers** cross North America. She led the group while caring for her new baby.

The explorers were led by Meriwether Lewis and William Clark.

On the journey, the group met many Native American **tribes**. Sacagawea helped everyone have peaceful talks. She was a big reason her group was able to travel safely.

**Be Inspired!** Try to bring people together as friends.

# DAVID LIVINGSTONE

**Born: 1813   Died: 1873**

David Livingstone was a doctor from Scotland. He spent many years exploring Africa. He first became famous when he crossed the middle of Africa from coast to coast.

Then, David went to find the start of the the Nile River. This is the world's longest river. The trip took so long some people thought he died. But he was just exploring.

**Be Inspired!**
Keep looking for new adventures.

# NELLIE BLY

**Born: 1864**
**Died: 1922**

Nellie Bly was an American **journalist**. She had read a novel about someone traveling the world in 80 days. She believed she could do it faster.

Nellie set off on her trip. She went on trains, ships, and even donkeys. She traveled around the world in just 72 days!

**Be Inspired!** Have **confidence** in yourself.

# GERTRUDE BELL

**Born: 1868**
**Died: 1926**

Gertrude Bell was a British woman who traveled the world. She was not afraid of going to new places, even when she was the only woman around.

Gertrude learned new things wherever she went. She dug up things from people who lived a long time ago. Gertrude wrote about many of the amazing things she found.

**Be Inspired!**

Never stop looking for things to learn about.

# ANNIE LONDONDERRY

**Born: 1870**
**Died: 1947**

Annie Londonderry was an American woman who decided to ride a bicycle around the world. When Annie set off, people thought she would not be able to do it.

Annie's heavy bicycle and long skirt gave her a slow start. Instead of giving up, she got a lighter bicycle and a pair of men's pants. She became the first woman to bike around the world!

**Be Inspired!** Try to solve a problem before giving up on it.

# ROALD AMUNDSEN

**Born: 1872**
**Died: 1928**

A Norwegian man named Roald Amundsen and his team were the first to get to the most southern place on Earth. They made it through difficult weather all the way to the South Pole.

Roald and his team knew they would have to travel in the freezing cold, so they prepared well. They dressed in warm clothes and rode **dogsleds** over the ice.

Be Inspired!

Don't be afraid to be the first!

# EDMUND HILLARY AND TENZING NORGAY

**Born:** 1919  **Died:** 2008    **Born:** 1914  **Died:** 1986

Edmund Hillary was from New Zealand

Tenzing Norgay was a **Sherpa** from Nepal

Edmund Hillary and Tenzing Norgay were the first people to climb to the top of Mount Everest. The two teamed up for the dangerous trip to the world's highest point.

At the top of Mount Everest, the adventurers faced many difficult things. The air was hard to breathe. It was so cold they had to melt ice from their boots before they could wear them!

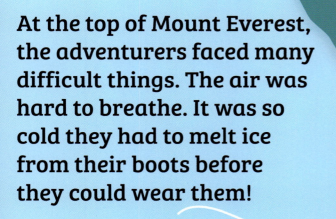

**Be Inspired!**

It's okay to get help when things are difficult.

# YOUR LAND ADVENTURE

There have been some great adventures over land. From riding in a dogsled to traveling by train, people have found wonderful ways to explore the world.

There are so many exciting places and things you can discover for yourself. If you could explore anywhere in the world, where would you go? Pick a place and plan your land adventure!

- Backpack
- Compass
- Hiking boots
- Map
- Warm clothes
- Water bottle
- Sunscreen

Write a list of everything you would need for your travels.

# GLOSSARY

**buried** put in a hole in the ground and then covered

**confidence** a sense of belief in one's ability to do something

**dogsleds** small, flat sleds pulled by groups of dogs

**emperor** a person who rules over an area of land and its people

**European** a person who is from a country in Europe

**explorers** people who travel to discover something new

**journalist** someone who writes news stories

**passport** a document that says where you are from and allows you to get into another country

**Sherpa** a person who is from a group in the Himalaya mountains that is known for helping other mountain climbers

**tribes** groups of people who live together

# INDEX

**Africa** 10
**American** 8–9, 12, 16
**bicycle** 16–17
**buried** 15

**camel** 7
**China** 6–7
**cold** 19, 21
**dogsled** 19, 22

**Mount Everest** 20–21
**Nile River** 11
**South Pole** 18